juices
and tonics

juices and tonics

elsa petersen-schepelern

photography by william lingwood

RYLAND
PETERS
& SMALL

Senior Designer Louise Leffler
Food Editor and Food Stylist Elsa Petersen-Schepelern
Editor Maddalena Bastianelli
Production Patricia Harrington
Photographer's Assistant Carl Davis
Art Director Gabriella Le Grazie
Publishing Director Anne Ryland

Acknowledgments

My thanks to my sister Kirsten, to Louise Leffler for her mouthwatering design, and to William Lingwood for his wonderful photographs. Waring very kindly provided their legendary blender and their muscular juicing machine for testing and shooting. Thanks also to Michael van Straten, my friend and former colleague from LBC Newstalk Radio in London, who is always so sensible about nutrition and complementary medicine. My brother-in-law, Ron Bray of Kallangur, Queensland, Australia, provided ongoing advice on the nutritional content and farming peculiarities of all manner of fruits and vegetables. Friend and colleague Maddy Bastianelli helped with research. Bhavin's Tropical Produce of Tooting, London, produced wonderful Asian fruits, while Leena Foods of Northcote Road in Battersea sought out the freshest spices in London.

First published in Great Britain in 2000
by Ryland Peters & Small, Cavendish House,
51–55 Mortimer Street, London W1N 7TD

10 9 8 7 6 5 4 3 2 1

Printed and bound in China by Toppan Printing Co.

ISBN 1 84172 051 8

A CIP record for this book is available from the British Library.

Notes

All spoon measurements are level unless otherwise stated.

All fruits and vegetables used in this book should be washed thoroughly and peeled in the usual way, unless otherwise advised. Carrots in particular should be peeled, topped, and tailed, and apples and pears should be cored before juicing. Unwaxed citrus fruits and cucumbers should be used whenever possible.

contents

introduction

Medical authorities maintain that we should have at least five servings of fruit and vegetables per day. I don't know about you, but three or four is as many as I normally manage. What better way to increase your uptake of healthful foods than to have them in juice form.

Which juicer? There are many kinds of juicer on the market, from the humble lemon squeezer (hard to improve on, really) to state-of-the-art extractors. Which should you choose? It depends on your budget, and perhaps even the size of your family or if you're a vegetarian. My own view is that you should get the best and strongest you can afford, and large enough so that you're not tempted to put it away in a cupboard and forget about it. Big is beautiful, and it will stay out on the kitchen counter. Mine has two separate mechanisms—one for citrus and one for everything else.

How long can you keep juice? No time at all. If you squeeze fresh orange juice and put it in a pitcher, it will start to separate in a matter of moments. The whole point of freshly squeezed juice is to drink it straight away. So do. Oxidization starts to happen within minutes, depending on the kind of juice. Think of an apple and how quickly that turns brown. It's still edible, but it's better for you and tastes better if you juice it and drink it immediately. That way, all the antioxidants in the juice will busily mop up any excess free radicals in the body—those "baddies" that cause cell damage.

How many ingredients? I think the fewer the better. If you add too many flavors, they all start to meld together and taste a little like fruity mud. Some juices however, like beetroot and spinach, are good for you in small quantities, but not so good (and not so nice) in large dollops. So mix the small doses of goodies with "extenders" like apple or orange juice.

Sweet and salt? There's no denying, fruits these days don't often get a chance to ripen on the tree, so are distinctly sour. You can add sugar of course (or honey, which is really just sugar) but the best way in my opinion is to add apple juice, nature's sweetener. And some vegetable juices really do need a pinch of salt to point up their flavors. But if you don't approve of salt, add a squeeze of lemon juice, which will do much the same thing.

In the case of fruits and vegetables that discolor quickly, add a squeeze of citrus juice to slow down the process.

So, to increase your vitamin intake, juicing is a great idea. You can always freeze the leftover juices and use them to chill drinks, or churn them into sorbets, or cook them in soups—which, incidentally, is an excellent use for the pulp left over after juicing, as is baking.

Tonics from herbs and spices Herbs and spices are age-old ways to flavor food and to gently influence body and mind. Rosemary tea will wake you up; lavender tea will help you nod off. Ordinary tea (which is, after all, just another kind of herb) will spark you up. Cardamom and ginger will calm an upset stomach; star anise and lemon are simply comforting. All are delicious ways to increase your liquid intake—and NONE of us gets enough of that!

fruits

Health Note: **Apples** are an important source of vitamin C and are used to combat fluid retention and constipation. They are particularly good for the heart and vascular system and can help to lower cholesterol levels. **Mint** helps digestion and **ginger** will calm an upset stomach.

apple

Minty Ginger Granny Smith

Any apples will do, but unpeeled Granny Smiths produce the most beautiful green. The ginger is optional, but utterly delicious, and the mint leaves make an even brighter green. Just a hint—we professional dieters know to use apple juice instead of sugar to add sweetness. Lime juice will stop the apple juice turning brown so quickly, but drink this concoction immediately—don't let it hang around, or you lose all the benefits of freshly crushed juice.

4 Granny Smiths, cored but not peeled, then cut into chunks
a chunk of fresh ginger, peeled and sliced
4–8 sprigs of mint
1 tablespoon fresh lime juice (optional)
Serves 1

Push half the apples through the tube, then the ginger, mint, and lime juice, if using, then the remaining apples.

Variation: Frozen Apple Margarita
Put 1 cup crushed ice into a blender, add the juice, and blend to a froth. The Margarita is ready when the sound of the motor changes—that means the mixture has risen away from the blades.

Pomegranate Squeeze

Pomegranates have an intriguing sweet-tart flavor and a color straight out of the Arabian Nights. In the Middle East and Pakistan, the fruit are grapefruit-sized, a deep purple-red, with juice to match. Grenadine syrup or liqueur is made from pomegranates.

3 pomegranates
1 orange (optional)
1 tablespoon grenadine (optional)
Serves 1

Cut the pomegranates in half around the middle. Using a lemon squeezer, squeeze the juice from the pomegranates and orange. Add grenadine, if using, then serve over ice.

pomegranate

Health Note: **Pomegranates** are very low in calories, but rich in phosphorus—important for building good bones and absorbing nutrients. Their sweet-tart flavor is very refreshing in hot weather. Mix them with orange juice for a slightly sweeter drink, and don't press the seeds too hard, or bitter flavors will be released.

Health Note: Like apples, **pears** are a gentle digestive and helpful in lowering cholesterol. They are high in potassium, which regulates blood pressure, and rich in vitamins C, B1, and B2. In combination with **ginger**, pears will help calm the digestion as well as tasting wonderful.

pears

Gingered Pear Juice

Commercially produced pear juice is delicious—but when freshly squeezed, especially over ice, it's out of this world. There also seems to be a particular affinity between pears and ginger. Pears must be eaten on the day they become ripe—left longer, their texture becomes "sleepy". Juicing is their savior.

2–3 pears, quartered and cored
a piece of fresh ginger, peeled
**   and sliced**
Serves 1

Juice 1 pear, then the ginger, then the remaining pear or pears. Serve immediately.

pineapple

Health Note: Fresh **pineapple** contains the enzyme bromelian, which helps with digestion. In fact it makes short work of fats and proteins, so is very good for dieters. It is soothing for sore throats, coughs, and upset stomachs.

**1 large pineapple, peeled, quartered,
  cored and cut in wedges**
juice of 1 lemon
To serve:
ice cubes
4 passionfruit
sugar or honey, to taste
Serves 4

Pineapple Crush

Put the pineapple through the juicer, add the lemon juice, and pour into a pitcher of ice. Stir in the flesh and seeds of 3 passionfruit and top with the remainder. Depending on the sweetness and ripeness of the pineapple, you may like to add a little sugar or honey.

Health Note: All fruits contain vitamin C, but oranges remain the benchmark against which all others are measured. Vitamin C is vital for life and fresh fruit and juice is the best way of getting it. Commercial juices are often pasteurized or heat-treated to sterilize and preserve them. Heat destroys vitamin C, so manufacturers replace it in the form of Ascorbic Acid. Remember, real fruit contains real vitamins.

orange

Apricot, Berry, and Orange

Apricots are very dense, so you may like to pulp them in the blender rather than putting them through the juicer. If you do decide to juice, remove the skins first*, and juice them alternately with pieces of apple.

8 ripe apricots, halved and pitted, then coarsely chopped
8 strawberries, hulled and halved
juice of 2 oranges
Serves 1

Put the apricots, strawberries, and orange juice in a blender. Blend until smooth, adding water if needed. (If the mixture is too thick, add a few ice cubes and blend again.)

*To remove the skins, bring a saucepan of water to a boil, then blanch the apricots for about 1 minute. Remove and pull off the skins with the back of a knife.

Blueberries and Orange

4 oranges
1 basket blueberries (about 3 cups)
Serves 1–2

Squeeze the oranges, then put the juice in a blender with the berries and blend until smooth. Alternatively, I often peel the oranges, then chop them up and feed half through a juicer, followed by the blueberries, then the remaining oranges.

Strawberries and Balsamic

Balsamic, the rich, slightly sweet, aged vinegar from Italy, should be used in moderation—use it like a spice, don't pour it in like ordinary vinegar. It also has an extraordinary affinity with strawberries. Rinse the berries before hulling, or they will fill with water.

2 baskets ripe strawberries
1 tablespoon honey (optional)
balsamic vinegar, to serve
Serves 2–4

Reserve a few strawberries for decoration, then put the remainder in a blender with the honey, if using, and a cupful of ice cubes. Purée adding water if necessary to make the mixture easier to blend. Purée again, then serve over ice, with a halved strawberry on top. Serve the balsamic separately, in drops.

strawberries

Health Note: Strawberries, like many other berries, help protect against cancer. The juice can also be used in small quantities combined with other juices, or to flavor yogurt drinks.
Vinegar is an aid to digestion, prevents fatigue, and lessens the risk of high blood pressure.

melon

Health Note: Melons are perfect for dieters, being mostly water, and make delicious juices. They move quickly and gently through the system, and are best eaten at the beginning of a meal rather than the end.

Melon Froth

These melon varieties are my favorites—very aromatic. My juicer produces a froth, but if yours is less muscular, you could layer the melon juices to form orange and green stripes. Wonderful for a summer lunch party.

1–2 melons—orange cantaloupe, or green honeydew, halved, seeded, and peeled
ginger syrup, from a jar of preserved ginger (optional)
Serves 1–2

Put the melons through a juicer. Layer the colors in glasses if preferred, or serve separately. Serve ginger syrup separately, if using.

Watermelon and Lime Slush

red flesh from 1 round watermelon
a piece of fresh ginger, grated
To serve:
2 limes, cut into wedges
crushed ice
Serves 4

Press the melon and ginger through a juicer,
then pour into a pitcher half full of crushed
ice. Serve immediately in chilled glasses with
lime wedges or use to make sorbet.
If serving as a sorbet, add sugar to taste (the
mixture should be very sweet), then churn in
an ice cream machine. Alternatively, partially
freeze in metal trays, then blend in a food
processor and freeze again. Just before
serving, crush into an icy slush.

watermelon

Health Note: **Watermelons** are mostly water, so they are refreshing and very good for dieters. The succulent flesh is high in vitamin C. **Limes**, also high in vitamin C, are good for pointing up the flavor, preserving the color, and slowing down the oxidization process. But don't wait around—juice and drink as soon as possible. Alternatively, churn and freeze, then serve as a slush.

Mexican Golden Salsa Crush

These three vegetables originally came from Mexico. I am not very fond of fiery-hot chiles, so one medium-hot one is perfect for me. Add more if you like, or use a hotter one. The pinch of salt is optional, but salt points up the flavors beautifully.

You could also use a dash of lemon juice instead. The real, raw juice is sweet enough.

1–2 red, orange or yellow bell peppers, halved and seeded
1 medium-hot red chile, seeded
2 tomatoes, quartered
a pinch of salt (optional) or a squeeze of lemon juice
Serves 1

Feed half the peppers into the juicer, then the chile, tomato, remaining peppers, and a pinch of salt, if using, or lemon juice.

vegetables

bell pepper

Health Note: Bell peppers and their hot-headed **chile** cousins have three times as much vitamin C as an orange. Juicing removes the indigestible skins and extracts all the sweet flavor.

Health Note: **Beets,** famous as a blood tonic, are a powerhouse of vitamins and minerals—A, B group, and C, plus calcium, iron, and potassium. Beets are good for blood pressure, protect against anemia, and promote general good health.

beets

Beet and Orange

Raw beet is good for you, but only in small quantities—and it has a decidedly earthy taste. Trimming and peeling before juicing will help, but best of all is "stretching" it with freshly squeezed juice such as orange or even apple. Depending on the sweetness of the oranges, you may need to add little honey.

1 medium beet, trimmed and peeled if preferred
2–3 oranges
honey, to taste
Serves 1

Cut the beet into pieces and press through a juicer. Squeeze the oranges. Stir well, then taste, adding honey if necessary.

Note: Beet leaves are also delicious. Either juice them separately or with spinach leaves—or sauté in a little olive oil and serve as an accompaniment to entrées.

fennel

Health Note: Like celery, fennel bulbs are low in calories and traditionally have been used to combat indigestion. **Fennel** contains beta carotene and folate, an important ingredient for pregnant women. **Apples** help maintain a healthy immune system.

Fennel can be very difficult to juice—
you need a powerful machine.
Alternatively, chop it and purée in a
blender with apple juice, then strain.
Use a crisp, sweet apple such as Red
Delicious to give a wonderful pinkish
tinge. Always remember to remove
the stem and stalk ends of apples and
pears, where any pesticides and
residues collect.

**1 fennel bulb, including sprigs of the
feathery leaves
2 apples, cored but not peeled
juice of ½ lemon (optional)
Serves 1–2**

Trim the green leaves from the fennel bulb,
trim off the root end, then slice the bulb into
long wedges and cut out and remove the
cores from each wedge. Cut the apple into
wedges. Put both through a juicer.
Stir in the lemon juice to stop discoloration,
then serve immediately, topped with a few
fennel sprigs for extra scent.

Fennel and Apple

Celery and Grapes

Celery juice is marvelous when mixed with other vegetable juices—but also with juicy fruits such as grapes. You can buy grape juice, but fresh juice is a revelation. White grapes will produce a fresh green juice—red or black ones a delicious pink-tinged nectar.

6 celery stalks, trimmed
about 20 seedless white grapes
1 bunch watercress (optional)
ice cubes
Serves 1–2

Push the celery stalks into the juicer, leaf end first. Alternate with the grapes, which are very soft and difficult to push through on their own. Press through the watercress, if using, and serve plain, in glasses filled with ice, or zapped with ice cubes in a blender to produce a delicious celery-grape froth.

Health Note: Celery has almost no calories—it's like eating water, so is marvelous for dieters. All fruits and vegetables contain phytochemicals which help the body fight disease —but celery is especially good for people who have gout, rheumatism, or high blood pressure. Celery is a natural tranquilizer and helps relieve fluid retention. Celery and grapes help protect against arthritis and gout, and alleviate joint pains. (Grapes are always good mixed with other juices.)

celery

Lettuce and Parsley Crush

Lettuce and parsley produce small quantities of juice and taste decidedly green! So add the juice of an apple or other fruit as an extender and sweetener. As many good cooks know, much of the flavor in parsley is in the stalks, so juice them too. Before juicing, all leafy vegetables should be washed well, wrapped in a cloth, and refrigerated until crisp.

1 romaine or iceberg lettuce, stalk trimmed
1 large bunch of parsley, including stalks, ends trimmed
1 green apple, cored but not peeled
Serves 1

Form the lettuce and parsley leaves into balls and push through the juicer. Lastly, to extract more juice, press an apple through. Stir if necessary, then serve immediately—don't wait.

parsley

Health Note: **Parsley** is famous as a breath freshener and an effective digestive. **Lettuce** is high in antioxidants, which prevent infection and protect against some cancers, heart disease, and premature aging. Both ingredients discolor quickly after being cut, so juice them and drink immediately. Dark-green leafy vegetables contain beneficial folic acid and bioflavonoids, so use the greenest variety of lettuce you can, such as romaine. The iceberg is a particularly juicy variety.
Make an infusion of parsley as a hair rinse to make your hair shiny.

cucumber

Health Note: Cucumber is
low in calories but rich in
vitamins B1, B2, and C and
minerals calcium and iron.
It is a natural diuretic.
Raw spinach, though good
for you, should not be taken
in very large doses. It
contains oxalic acid which
locks up other vitamins so
they can't be used by the
body. In spite of its Popeye
reputation, spinach isn't
particularly high in iron.
When it was retested in the
1940s, it was found that
someone had put the decimal
point in the wrong place!

Cucumber and Spinach

Yes, spinach is good for you—but too much isn't. Spinach juice is also no-one's idea of a good time, but mix it with something more delicious and you'll absorb all its goodness almost painlessly. Take care—cucumbers are often waxed, but organically grown produce won't be. If you can find only the waxed kind, you'll have to peel them and so lose most of the color and many of the nutrients.

1 organic cucumber, about 12 inches long, quartered lengthwise
1 large handful well-washed spinach
salt or lemon juice, to taste (optional)
Serves 1–2

Juice half the cucumber, then all the spinach, then the remaining cucumber. Add salt or lemon juice to taste, if using.

Variation:
Cucumber has a cooling, astringent effect—to sweeten it, use half-and-half with apple juice from crisp Granny Smiths.

carrot

Health Note: Carrots are high in beta carotene, which the body uses to convert into vitamin A. The nutrients are easier to digest when cooked, but carrot juice is utterly delicious. Don't have this drink more than twice a week, or you run the risk of developing an orange tinge to your skin!

Carrot and Ginger Crush

Carrot juice, so naturally sweet, is my
absolutely favorite juice. Though
carrots are better for you when
cooked, I much prefer them raw. Just
make sure you peel them first, unless
they have been organically grown.

5 medium carrots, peeled
a piece of fresh ginger, peeled and
   sliced (optional)
Serves 1–2

Cut the carrots into pieces small enough to
fit through the juicer tube. When half the
carrots have been processed, add the ginger,
if using, then the rest of the carrots.

Fresh Virgin Mary

Make Bloody Mary with fresh juices and your friends will love you forever. Fresh tomato juice is thinner and sweeter than the commercial kinds—and more delicious.

6 ripe tomatoes
3 celery stalks
1 garlic clove (optional)
1 red chile, seeded
ice cubes
a dash of Worcestershire sauce (optional)
Serves 1

To skin the tomatoes, cut a small cross in the base, put into a large bowl and cover with boiling water. Leave for 1 minute, then drain and pull off the skins. Juice the tomatoes, celery, garlic (if using) and chilli. Pour into a jug of ice, stir in the Worcestershire sauce, if using, then serve (with or without vodka).

Variations: Add other fruit and vegetable juices such as broccoli, cabbage, lemon, or radish—and a dash of Moroccan harissa paste.

Health Note: The **tomato** is probably the world's single most wonderful vegetable (though it's technically a fruit). Tomatoes are low in calories but high in vitamins C and E, plus potassium, beta carotene, and lycopene, which helps some forms of cancer by preventing damage by free radicals. **Garlic** is one of nature's medicines, lowering cholesterol and blood pressure, protecting against cancer, soothing coughs and colds, and aiding digestion. It also contains polyphenols, which protect the heart.

French tisanes are infusions of herbs, flowers, or leaves, usually dried. I prefer them made with fresh ingredients where possible. In early, times, they were seen as cures for many ailments. Nowadays, people drink them because they taste good. A *tisanière* is a tall, lidded cup, with a strainer inside to hold the herb. If you don't have one (they are to be found in antique shops), use a French press or teapot instead.

4–6 sprigs of rosemary
1–2 teaspoons honey
Serves 1–2

Put the rosemary and honey in a French press or teapot, cover with boiling water, let infuse for about 5 minutes, then plunge or strain.

Variations: Tisanes are also made with camomile flowers, lemon balm, marjoram, sage, thyme, and orange blossoms.

Rosemary Tisane

teas and tisanes

**Health Note:
Rosemary** tea will
wake you up, so
drink it only in
the morning (it's
also good for
a hangover).
Do not use while
pregnant or when
breast-feeding.

rosemary

Health Note: Cardamom **and ginger** help with indigestion, nausea, coughs, and colds. Brew them, separately or together, in tea or coffee, with or without milk. Tea, especially **green tea**, is high in bioflavonoids—the antioxidants that help protect against heart disease and cancer.

cardamom

Cardamom Green Tea

An idea from Pakistan, which makes the world's most wonderful tea: a pot of green tea contains an aromatic treasure—a spoonful of green cardamom pods. Cardamom and ginger are both powerful soothing agents for upset stomachs.

1 teaspoon green tea, plus 1 for the pot
6 green cardamom pods
sugar, to taste
Serves 2

Rinse the teapot with boiling water, add the tea and cardamom, then fill with boiling water. Let steep for 1–2 minutes only (no longer, or the bitter tannins are released). Pour the tea and add sugar only if you usually like sweet tea.

1 large bunch of mint
sugar or honey, to taste (optional)
1 tablespoon green tea (optional)
Serves 1–4

Wash the mint well, then break it in large handfuls and put into a French press.
Pour over boiling water, let steep for 3–5 minutes, then press the plunger. Pour into tea
glasses, add honey, if using, and a few fresh mint leaves, then serve. If using green tea, add it
at the same time as the mint.

Mint Tea

Health Note: **Mint** is a stimulant, so don't drink it late at night. It will help digestion and relieve an upset stomach. Do not use while pregnant or when breast-feeding.

mint

Lavender Tea

The very essence of a hot summer afternoon in Italy or the South of France, lavender tea is very calming— good to drink before bed.

1–2 branches lavender leaves
a few lavender flowers, if available
1 teaspoon honey, or to taste
Serves 1

Put the lavender in a teapot or one-cup French press coffee pot and and cover with boiling water. Put on the lid and let steep for about 5 minutes.
Put 1 teaspoon honey, if using, in your cup, then press the plunger and pour the tea. Alternatively, pour the honey over the lavender in the French press before adding the boiling water.

lavender

Health Note:
Lavender is a
decongestant,
general tonic, and
immunity booster.
It is mildly
sedative, so it
is good to drink
before bed or when
you need to relax.
It is also very
soothing for
people prone
to overwork.

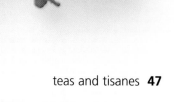

lemons and limes

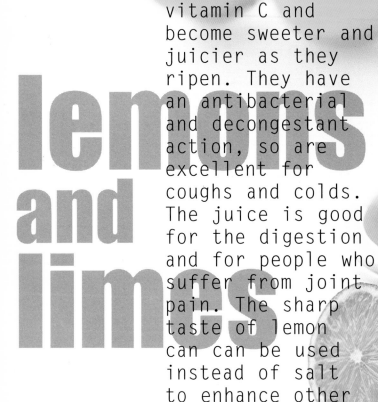

Health Note:
Lemons and limes
are high in
vitamin C and
become sweeter and
juicier as they
ripen. They have
an antibacterial
and decongestant
action, so are
excellent for
coughs and colds.
The juice is good
for the digestion
and for people who
suffer from joint
pain. The sharp
taste of lemon
can can be used
instead of salt
to enhance other
flavors.

**4 cups freshly made tea, lightly
  brewed**
sugar, to taste
1–2 unwaxed limes, finely sliced
ice cubes
mineral water, lemonade, or gingerale
Serves 4

Strain the tea, stir in the sugar, then cool and
chill. Put sliced limes in a pitcher, then half-fill
it with ice cubes. Half-fill the jug with the
cold tea, then top up with mineral water,
lemonade, or gingerale, stir, and serve.

Iced Lime Tea

1 unwaxed lemon
1 pot of tea
1 tablespoon honey
Serves 1

Cut 2 slices off the lemon and squeeze the
juice from the rest. Put the honey and sliced
lemon in a large mug, add the lemon juice,
then top with tea. Stir and drink.

Hot Lemon Tea with Honey

If you like aniseed flavors, like licorice or pastis, you'll love this drink. Tea is always best made with leaves, but this recipe can also be made with your favorite brand of tea bag. I like it best not too strong and served without milk.

1 tea bag, such as English Breakfast
1 whole star anise
sweetener, to taste
milk (optional)
Serves 1

Put the tea bag and star anise in a cup, add sweetener if you usually use it, then add boiling water. Add milk if preferred. Let steep for your usual amount of time, then remove the tea bag and serve.

Star Anise Tea

Health Note: Star anise is a delicious breath freshener. It also stimulates the appetite and calms a growling tummy. It can act both as a stimulant and as a sedative. Tea, especially **green tea,** is high in antioxidants, which help the body protect itself against heart disease and cancer.

star anise

ginger

Health Note: Ginger is an all-purpose tonic. It is astonishing in its ability to calm an upset stomach, can help ease the pain of arthritis and indigestion, and soothes coughs and headcolds.

Ginger Tea

a piece of fresh ginger
1 teaspoon leaf tea (optional)
sweetener of your choice
Serves 1

Peel and grate the ginger. (The cheese-grater shown here is quick, clean, and easy.) Put in a tea strainer or tea ball, then add the tea, if using. Put the ball in the cup or balance the strainer over the cup. Add boiling water and let steep for 1–5 minutes, according to how strong you like the flavor. Add sweetener if you like, then sip slowly. The same ginger can be used for extra cups.

Almond Milk

Nut milks are delicious for people who "don't do dairy".
You can make them with any nuts, but almonds are easy to
find. You can use unblanched almonds (with their skins still
on), but the result is browner and grittier. To blanch your
own almonds, put in a bowl, cover with boiling water,
leave for 5 minutes, then pop them out of their skins.

1 package almonds, preferably blanched (about ¾ cup)
1 tablespoon honey
1 cup ice cubes or crushed ice
Serves 1

Put the almonds and honey in a blender, add the ice cubes, and
1 cup ice water. Blend to a paste. Gradually add extra ice water until
the mixture is smooth. Strain and serve over ice.

Note: The process can be repeated several times, producing thinner
and thinner "milk" each time. Eventually, the strained almond meal
can be used to thicken sauces or flavor breads, cakes, or cookies.

nut milks
and yogurt

nuts

Health Note: Almond milk is a classic invalid food, a true tonic. All nuts are high in protein (important for vegetarians) and in oils. They also contain vitamin E—a powerful antioxidant—which is more beneficial in foods, rather than in pill form. Almonds also contain minerals such as zinc, magnesium, potassium, calcium, and iron.

mango

Health Note: Eating ripe fresh **mangoes** is good for the skin and for people with high blood pressure. Mangoes are better blended rather than juiced and are good mixed with other ingredients, such as coconut milk or yogurt. Take care when peeling them, and don't eat the flesh straight from·the peel, because sap from the stem and peel can cause blisters. (When a mango is properly ripe, you should be able to pull the peel off the fruit as shown. If you have to use a knife, it's not ripe.)

Mango and Coconut Milk

Another nut-milk recipe, particularly good for people who are lactose-intolerant—and for anyone lucky enough to have too many mangoes.

**2 fresh ripe mangoes, peeled and
   pitted, or 1 cup mango purée
juice of ½ lime or lemon
1 cup desiccated coconut (measured by
   volume), or canned coconut milk
Serves 2**

Blend the mangoes with the lime or lemon juice, then transfer to a pitcher and chill. If using desiccated coconut, put it in a blender with 1 cup ice water. Blend until frothy, let stand for 5 minutes, then blend again. Strain into the pitcher and return the coconut to the blender. Repeat with another cup of ice water. Strain, then stir into the pitcher of mango and lime or lemon, then serve. Alternatively, omit the coconut milk and just blend the mango and lime or lemon juice with enough ice cubes and water to make a pourable consistency.

Fruit Ice Cubes with Buttermilk Froth

Freeze a selection of fresh juices in an ice cube tray and serve with buttermilk for a delicious breakfast on a hot day.

1 tray ice cubes made of fruit juices
½ cup buttermilk or low-fat yogurt
sparkling mineral water or seltzer
Serves 4

Fill 4 glasses with the fruity ice cubes, add 2 tablespoons buttermilk or yogurt, then top with sparkling mineral water or seltzer. The ice cubes melt slowly into the drink, so you can top it up with more buttermilk or more mineral water for a long, cool, delicious, and filling drink.

buttermilk

Health Note: Traditionally, **buttermilk** was the part of the milk left when all the fats (butters) had been churned away. Modern buttermilks are simply skim milks with a light culture, similar to yogurt, added. Mix it with icy fruit squeezes—ice cubes made from fruit juice melt more slowly than ordinary cubes—so they're good for a long, leisurely breakfast.
As with most milk products, buttermilk is high in calcium. It is also low in fat, while the bio-culture is good for the digestion.

banana

Health Note: Bananas are high in complex carbohydrates—that's why tennis players eat them at Wimbledon. Very nourishing and good for your cholesterol levels, they are high-energy foods, rich in potassium and vitamins A, C, and K. A meal in themselves, they are wonderful for breakfast and very good for growing children.

Papaya and Banana Smoothie

Papayas and bananas won't juice effectively—their pulp is too dense—but are definitely candidates for the blender treatment. If your blender doesn't crush ice, add it at the end, but, to help the machine run, you will need a little water, yogurt, or juice.

1 small papaya, peeled, seeded, and cut into chunks
1 banana, peeled and cut into chunks
1 cup ice
½ cup yogurt (optional)
1 tablespoon wheatgerm (optional)
Serves 2–4

Put the papaya and banana into a blender with the ice and ½ cup water or yogurt. Pulse until smooth, then add the wheatgerm, if using, and extra water or yogurt, if using, to form a pourable consistency.

Variation:
Blueberries and banana make a famous combination. Blend them with ice, yogurt, and a dash of honey, if preferred.

Red Berry Smoothie

Even people with dairy intolerance are often able to eat yogurt, since it changes its structure during fermentation. It's marvelous for people with upset stomachs too!

**1 punnet berries (about 2–3 cups),
such as strawberries, cranberries, red
currants, or raspberries (for a pink
smoothie) or blackberries and
blueberries (for a blue smoothie)**
1 cup plain yogurt
½ cup crushed ice
Serves 2–3

Put all the ingredients in a blender and work to a thin, frothy cream. If too thick, add water to create a pourable consistency.

berries

Health Note: **Berries** are high in vitamin C and antioxidants which protect against cancer and heart disease and help ease the pain of arthritis. A daily helping of 1 cup blueberries contains enough antioxidants to improve balance, coordination, and short-term memory. Strawberries also improve memory. Most berries are better blended rather than juiced, and are good mixed with other fruits or with yogurt in smoothies and lassis.

Plain low-fat yogurt is the best form of calcium for women and is helpful in treating digestive disorders.

index